Pressed Petals

Maverick L. Malone

Published by Argyle Fox Publishing | argylefoxpublishing.com

Publisher holds no responsibility for content of this work. Content is the sole responsibility of the author.

ISBN 978-1-953259-50-9

ARGYLE FOX
PUBLISHING

For Lilly

Not just a page in my story, but whole chapters;
never just petals, but entire flowers

Mission Statement

I want to be the proof that magic is real
a shimmering thing to be cultivated
that creativity and perspective
are the elixirs to discontent

I want to be an example
to always speak in italics (*emphasize your point!*)
use ellipses (leave them wanting more . . .)
dress like you're wearing poetry (lyrical beauty)
live in vivid color
and have the stories
memories
tattoos
wardrobe
and photographs to prove it

I want to be an asteroid impact
on the people ready to explode in the *best way possible*
to turn chaos into catharsis
and hardship into healing

I want to get to the end of my life
having spun a single thread of hope into a whole spool
left behind in a legacy of leather-bound words
for my daughter and anyone else
who finds the riddles of life
too challenging sometimes

I want to teach people to find their spark
and learn to see in the dark
and live their biggest and brightest lives
IN BOLDFACE TYPE

Preface

They say the relationships in *life* are a reflection, mirroring back to us what we usually can't see for ourselves. Writing works the same way. It *is* a two-way mirror. *In the moment*, you're just *in* the thick of it, the one interrogating yourself as you go, exploring *all of your parts unknown*. Often, you have no idea what the other side of that glass looks like, completely unaware of what may be staring you in the face the whole time. When you come to the end of a poem or *whatever* thing you've just written, it's as if you're on the other side of that mirror as the observer, able to peer at it lovingly and objectively for what it is, while other times, you are accosted with *your* own honesty and *truth*. The adventure therein lies in getting lost within those very words and waiting to see what may materialize.

Half the time I have no idea what I'm going to write when my fingers start typing or the pen starts moving. For me, it is the absolute apex of being present because nothing else exists when I'm in that space, getting naked on the page, just letting whatever *wants to* bless me with its presence *reveal* itself in the moment on paper. It is for this reason that I often say, "I don't manifest my books. My books manifest me."

Take this anthology for instance. I never set out to intentionally write it, but over time, as the notes on my phone grew to epic proportions, I realized what I had been doing over the span of a year and a half as I moved through some of the hardest moments of my life: I had been writing my first book. And throughout that process of creative writing, I was learning, changing, growing, and healing. Through the exploration of self, I was becoming.

There is such a deep catharsis in writing, which initially drew me back to it. I have always been a writer, but over time I lost that part of my identity. I was in so much pain that I had become numb to all of my emotions. Writing rescued me in the softest and subtlest way. It *is* my medicine, the remedy for chaos. The times I feel powerless or lost in life are the times when I feel most powerful on the page. It's how I explore things I don't understand or work out difficult emotions. It's escapism, time travel, therapy, and most of all . . . *magic*.

I began picking up poetry again as a way to explore those big feelings, not only about my crumbling marriage, but also who I was as a human being beyond the labels of "wife" *and* "mother," and in doing so, I was finally learning how to *love* myself. The poems I was penning *unveiled* my innermost desires and fostered an allowance of my deepest truth, luring it into the light. As I followed the proverbial rabbit further down, she led me to the decision that ultimately changed the entire trajectory of my future.

All I want from this first anthology is to preserve all of these petaled versions of myself *through* life—especially through the divorce—and to contemplate where I've been in order to better understand where I'm going. I am honored that you picked up this book to come along on that self-discovery and *healing* journey with me.

I have such a love affair with language—with alliteration, imagery, metaphors, and magic, and I can't keep it a secret any longer. I don't want you to just read my work. I want you to feel it. If even one person can feel connected, seen, understood, or loved through my work, then I have succeeded. If I can inspire someone else to chase their dream, pin it down, wear it like a badge of honor on their chest, and never let it out of their sight again, that's success.

In today's world, there is so much pain and despair projected out through the media machine that it's all too easy to fall prey to negativity and retreat back into the confines of safety we've carved out for ourselves. But that same world is also *brimming with beauty and possibility* if we just take a deep breath *and* jump.

The world is starving for light and if sharing the story of how I found my way back to it can help a kindred spirit in need, then that is the best return on investment I could ask for. *That is a story worth telling.*

The Poem in the Preface

Life is in the moment
in all of your parts unknown

whatever your truth wants to reveal
is magic and love unveiled through healing
brimming with beauty and possibility

and that is a story worth telling.

Pressed Petals

I press flowers
each petal another layer of truth
peeled back gingerly from the pistil
the verities of self perfectly preserved
between the pages in latently layered words

love fortunes scrawled
on the underside of daisies
a lotus rebirth at midnight
caught in fragmented phrases
magnolia promises emerging
from the sharpest end of a thought
a blast of resilient sunflowers
these compasses of light

truth—
both the flower and the bee
the bramble and the fruit
exposed vulnerability
that stings and soothes and flourishes

careful
not to weed my garden too much
that I completely miss the point of thorns

Moonflower

The stories I tell in the dark
are the ones that come true
that want to know
only light

I will carry them
until they can taste the sun

Pardon the Interruption

Allow me to regale you with a little bit of backstory for this next piece. It was written at age 19, circa 2007 during my sophomore year of college and the beginning of my relationship with my now ex-husband (as of 2022). You do the math.

Prior to meeting him, I used to write all the time. I would get carried off on a silver strand of thought so easily that I never knew where (or when) I would land. I would draw, paint, and write in any and every moment I could catch with my two hands. That was before everything changed.

I was swept up in the kind of romance I had always dreamed of, the stuff of fairy tales, and it was magical, wonderful, and beautiful. Until it wasn't.

I stopped writing. Over time, a part of me slipped away quietly, as if I no longer needed her. Another part of me became molded like clay in this other person's image and ideals. I became so entangled with this other person that the one part of myself that I had always been the most connected to seemed to disappear overnight.

So here I am, pressing this one into the book like a withered flower, in all her muted-hued beauty. I am pressing this one into the book as an homage to that version of myself that (maybe on some level) knew what was coming. I am pressing this one into the book to honor *her* because even though she stopped writing for years, she never let go of wild hope.

Who Am I if Not an Artist

The suction of that charred black space
born from the absence of the muse
fills me up
this pressure
this pulse
this, *THIS*
escapism bottled in tiny vials
marked "inspiration"
"epiphanies"
"artistic vision"

all

e   m   p   t   y   n   o   w

leaving a heap of this addict babbling into the dark
where I find nothing left to cling to
but letters to a questionable god
and the frail being of my inner soul
the sanctuary of my heart
that once beat with metronomic poetry
now lays still, dormant
in this blank canvassed flesh of a body

I must have lost it somewhere
along the red line marked from start to finish
like a children's maze game
torn haphazardly from a coloring book
on a night when I strayed too far from my post
as vigilante of the artist within
opting instead to be consumed
by an emotion I know nothing about

as if love would bring significance
would bring balance
would bring enlightenment
would bring the muse back to life

I must have lost her
to that damp black space riddled with crumpled paper
the kind scrawled out in class
with half-finished poems in the margins
the beginnings of genius sparked
while infant minds expanded
digesting knowledge
translating it into silver-lined coherence

think, *think!*

Where did I put it?

Have I unknowingly murdered the only part of me
I ever really understood?

Glow in the Dark Stars

I tell myself it's okay
when I'm the only one
that can hold my hand in the dark
slip between sheets
throw the covers over my head
and fall into a poem instead
shaping stars and planets
with incandescent ink
that stain my fingertips
the most perfect shade of peace
leaving behind an imprinted embrace
kind and familiar
trailing the promise of tomorrow
at the end of an ellipsis . . .

. . . sometimes
just the right words
feel a lot like love

Catharsis

I write
when the weather of the day
becomes too great
for my flimsy umbrella

so I fashion a house
out of words
to weather the storm
and find peace
among the rain

Bitter Indiscretion

The air smells stale
stifling
lingering with regret
laced with the sickeningly sweet
artificial reality of poor decisions
poured too often from glistening bottles
sipping satisfaction
swigged back from a highball glass
burning sweet liquid inspiration
coming to coat my veins yet again
just so I can feel
anything but the truth

yeah,
that smooth talker
knows all the right words to say
to get me in his bed

Reduction

Slowly
I coax them out
the words spilling forth
after too many glasses of wine
while the dishes bubble impatiently in the sink
and the wet clothes lie wholly forgotten in the wash
while the baby sleeps and the husband drinks
and the days run together in scheduled monotony
until sparks fly late at night
in a fury of a brilliant moment
catalytic reactions in the part of my mind
I thought had escaped out the trap door a decade ago
and stole off with my sanity into the weeping night

now bangs on the door, desperate,
begging me to let him in
and lay with him once again
to pen poems and recount the tales of my youth
shape words that seethe and stories that soothe
this Wild Fantastic with a gilded thread of truth

or maybe
mostly
to simply create
what we never had to begin with

If I Seem Off

If I seem off today
I'm trying to cover up the hurt
for what I thought was blooming
has been pressed back into dirt

if I seem off today
it's from the words we both have spoken

if I seem off today
it's because you said that I was
b   r   o   k   e

n

Until

I sat outside listening to the birds
until they transformed into crickets
until the sun went down
until the rustling settled into stillness
until the porch light glowed
until the stars came out
until the moon wove its wisdom
until night shaped peace in the silhouettes of trees
until the salt trailed down skin
until the hurt in my heart
felt a little
less

                      y
                v
           a
      e
  h

Disillusioned Dissolutions

I wanted to believe in us

at one time
I did

at one time I believed so desperately
that I filled an entire notebook
with love letters, quotes and songs
and cartoon doodles
of the way your smile looked in the morning
caught somewhere between worlds
of an unfolding fairy tale and a brittle-glass reality
that could break at any given moment
reducing me to shards of porcelain
cutting through the fleshy parts of a heart
with words like "promise"
"forever"
"us"

I don't know where those words are now
absent from my vocabulary
because certain plural pronouns
ceased to be a long time ago
and when I started picking myself first for gym class
something massively shifted
and the cosmos conspired to rewrite my destiny

I used to believe that our love
was the only love
and I burned hotter than the stars back then
back when I could feel the sun in my chest
sizzling from the inside
and my mind was a double feature of you
"Now (always) Playing"

at one time I believed in eternity so wholeheartedly
I would've ripped myself open
spilling all over the table
just to show you the ten-piece band in my heart
pounding out the rhythms of long ago love letters
that this
was
it
the stuff of legends and ancient mysteries
our own mythology
the spark in the dark of magnificent beginnings
the kiss that showed me your soul unfurling
the kind of love that had me speaking in tongues
only you could decipher
and your touch was a match that lit me aflame

yes,
once upon a time
we weren't just smoke and mirrors

(*After I wrote this in the car, I put my Spotify on shuffle and
a song called "Smoke and Mirrors" came on. I had chills. The
good kind. The Universe is always listening.)

You're Such a Doll, You Should Smile More

If days were dolls
then some feel
as if I am an 80's Stretch Armstrong
the head
each leg and arm
pulled in a different direction
never enough elasticity to last
snapping in a rubber band burn so fast
the sting begins to feel familiar

some days I am the Russian nesting doll
the largest and strongest facade
presented with a painted-on smile
hiding
—no—
protecting
her more vulnerable counterparts within

some days I am the voodoo doll
with tiny needles pinpointing
each exact imperfection with perfect precision
pushing that pain in a little deeper
just to make sure I'm still all there

some days find me
as nothing more than a rag doll
trailing along the dirty hallway floor
swept up in a visceral show of dust and debris
where my crude stitches rip loose
on the jagged edge of a rogue nail
and the stuffing falls out in a breadcrumb trail
back to the safety of a bedroom

sometimes I forget
that no matter how much the day toys with me
I will keep risking it all
just for a chance
to exist beyond the shelf

Fresh Ink

It happened by happenstance
the earth opening up beneath my feet
and I half wanted it to swallow me whole

it might have been easier that way—
I've never been much for combat

the words burn on the page
and churn in my mind
a tattoo of a different kind
invisible ink for invisible scars
materializing before me
but instead
I parcel out my peace
as penance for such ignorance

how long can I pretend this is enough for me?

Ships Passing

To be human
is a strange and complex thing

how can I sense you so close
pressed up against me
and yet
there is an ocean
between our bodies

to feel so lost
in the sea of us?

Replay

The record crackles around our static
so I lean in
let it play
as it scrambles the signals in my head
because I could never hurt you
so I sacrifice myself instead

Party of One

I pretended not to care
that it didn't hurt to be an afterthought
that I was content to sip solo and wait
the celebration of chips
and a half-drunk mango margarita
all alone at the table
but it says a lot about a partner
who shows up late to your birthday
when they were the only one invited

It's Always the Quiet Ones

It's ironic
you think I'm too quiet
when all the words I write are screams

The Wanderer

It's not my eyes
that wander

but rather my soul
that strays

Who & What Army?

When giving in
feels like giving up
and the darkness seethes red
with a slow-mo bass growl
that could shake a soul
I will always reach for the pen
and write myself out of the problem
for truth
is the most powerful defense
and I'm never short on ink

Distractions in Every Direction

I try to bury it sometimes
the hurt

dress it up
in beautiful beaded 60's gowns
and 50's tulle confections
anoint it in shimmer, glitter, and sparkle
allow it to deflect my attention

hide it behind heart-shaped shades
drown it in Cabernet
(sometimes whiskey
when it feels insurmountable)
sink it beneath the waves
of a tropical beach vacation

to keep running
past the point of exhaustion
in all directions at once
because hey
at least in all those fragmented moments
I felt alive
and forgot about the ache
for just a little while

The Lark Sings in Legato

This is not my swan song
staccato separated by silence
final tunes before the show
has even begun

I have many melodies
left to share
for my notes vibrate into the sunrise
from the throat of a lark
and if I ever want to reach the moon
I have to keep singing
through the dark

Beached

Is this it?

feet lingering at the shore
like an old familiar lover
stirrings of comfort and safety
lest I am carried off by the current
swept up into the tumultuous sea

I don't like that I can't see the bottom
the midnight blue overtaking my breath
gasping
swallowing too much seawater
waves breaking over my body
tossed into the eye of the storm
sucked down
unsure of when
or if
I may resurface

yet still
I am called
pulled
into the wild depths
in search of treasure and adventure
knowing that while the risk is great
cowardice would be far worse

and if my stories get lost at sea
at least I followed the siren song calling me

everything washes ashore eventually

Tempest

There's a storm coming,
and they don't know

it's me.

How It Ends

My head is a library
where thoughts of you
are filed away methodically

I alphabetize your behaviors
and reorganize your actions
place your love-laced words
gingerly petal-pressed
between the parchment pages of my heart

I revisit this library often
plucking books from the shelf
inhaling the scent of each memory:
the honeysuckle thick in the summer heat
and the wine you spilled on my dress
before you slipped it off
letting your hands wander
the unexplored territory of my body

I am a curator of reminiscence
a master of recollection
keeping only those remnants
that make the corners of my mouth turn up
in time with the wings vibrating in my chest
and the promise on your breath
reveling in disillusioned optimism
ignorant of the unyielding truth
that we were never built to last

Two Steps Back

Just when I thought I had bloomed
doubt and confusion
rip me out at the roots

On Second Thought

What do you do
when half of you wants to stay
and half of you wants to go?

Why does the head ignore
what the heart already knows?

Let Me Go

My hands are not strong enough
to hold both our pain

something has to give

Sit with It

Acknowledge it
this thing you've ignored

you don't have to keep secrets
from yourself anymore

Crown & Glory

Heavy is the head
bearing a crown of shining truth
unwilling
to ascend the throne

you were meant for
  s o
        m   u   c   h
                          m   o   r   e
than hiding in your tower

spires
in spite of yourself

holding court over mere pages

glory be!
a martyr unto only thee

I'm Fine

The first time around, I didn't feel safe enough to pull out the parts of me that were tucked away in an art box, brimming with raw truth; the parts of me that spilled over into notebooks and half-finished sketches; the parts of me that looked pretty on paper but were heavy, and dark, and deep; the parts of me that created a patchwork of my fleeting youth; the parts of me first measured in numbers on a scale followed by numbers on a screen; the parts of me that folded into a paper doll and became insatiable for bones; the parts of me cut the deepest by my own hand; the parts of me that reached into the depths of my heart just to touch the possibility of purpose; the parts of me that screamed and sang; the parts of me that measured self-worth in apothecary jars of other peoples' opinions and judgments; the parts of me that fell into the bottle to cover up the nights that ran so deep with thought that I had to drown in that poison just to escape myself; the parts of me that always remained hidden beneath a painted on smile.

I never felt safe enough to face my own shadows until you unraveled me so slowly over time that I lost my mind and had no choice but to rewind all the bullshit I thought was mine—to move backward to go forward, to dig deeper to get out, to fall to finally rise.

I never felt safe

until I stopped believing my own lies.

The Frequency of Running Water

My heart wrote a love letter to God
and switched over to autopilot
unbeknownst to me
as I lay sobbing on the shower floor
reflections of the me I used to be
looped continuously in my head
half of me
wanting to move back into that space
that safety
that familiarity
before this all began

but the heart
forever tethered to heaven
that wise seer in me
always knew the truth
and sent out the distress call in the frequency of love

a song came on like an S.O.S.
spoke above my sobs and assuaged my spirit
in vibrations and warm palms
wrapped around my shoulders
tenderly
softly
brought me to my feet

renewed
even for the moment
long enough
for me to remember the "why"
and keep going

Antiques

I sat with myself today
in my childhood room
the now-yellow walls
still pink and flowering in my mind
as she unzipped her chest
removed its contents
little baubles and trinkets she'd kept
like her body was just a wooden bureau
mine to borrow
holding everything I couldn't
until I was willing
to rifle through long enough
and release it

Unconditional

The clouds are swollen with the same water
as the dam ripping loose from my eyes
knowing you were never mine
in the way I needed you to be
in the way expectation had always toyed with me
in my astrology
in divine timing
a perfect storm of events
with not even enough notice to grab a raincoat

how lucky then
to wait out this tempest
from the shelter of my own syntax sanctuary
from the comforting embrace of a poem
that never asked for anything in return

How the Past Rests in Pieces

For the mistakes I made in so many varying shapes
for the slow simmer and inevitable boiling point of my temper
for priorities more mixed up
than all of my daughter's play dough mushed together
for how long it took to make space with a teaspoon
for raw salted tear-flavored cookie dough at midnight
for French kissing dysfunction
and locking awareness out of the house (again)
for wearing so many masks like every day is Carnival
for selling my self-worth to the highest bidder
for forgetting the friction of diction in the right direction
for driving with one foot on the gas
but continually pulling the E-break
for tears held back in a false narrative of misguided strength
for looking the wrong direction down a one-way street
for too many heavy-hitting Adele songs spinning on repeat
for bad habits born from the back roads of truth
shattered and frantically glued back together
for the things I said quietly under my breath
and for all the others
that never escaped my head

It is me
I forgive
for all this self-love
too far
misled

As a Matter of Dissatis(fact)ion

I yearn for growth
and new experiences
and the taste of courage

it's all just a matter of perspective—
the difference between being alone
and being on your own

so maybe the word "us"
is just something I've outgrown

Top Down, Bottoms Up

Your truth is showing.
GIRL!
you're growing
you're becoming
so keep going if you've made it this far
you already know who the fuck you are
you don't have to limit yourself to these tiny jars
one for work, one for home
when you're with him, when you're alone
just ask yourself this: does the truth still flow
When you stand in your power, all on your own

(Now read it from the last line first. Bottoms up!)

Lotus

*What's meant for me
will wait patiently
until I have bloomed enough
to rise through shadows to find it*

Your Blinker's Out

Dis co n n ec tio n
our **I**nfrastructure
couldn't withstand

such poor **V**isibility
from the passenger side

where you sat **O**blivious
to the weather again

too many right-hand turns on **R**ed
when we should have gone left
no recourse

in an ill-fated crash course **C**ollision

the only way out was through
the little death

at the dead **E**nd of me and you

Red Light

We absorbed each other
like darkroom chemicals
and still developed
overexposed

Eulogy

I needed something
you could not give
and so my heart broke
long before we ever did

Stay or Go

It was never a question
of me finding someone else
some unknown mysterious love
lingering beyond the veil
but rather
a personal search for inner strength
and a deep aching need
tugging at the hem of my soul
to know if I'm brave enough
to stand on my own

An Extended Phantasm

If I were the smoke and you were the mirror
it's no surprise
we believed our own illusion for so long

but that's the thing about smoke:
it dissipates
leaving the mirror no choice
but to reflect the truth

The Plans We Made

It's not
A L W A Y S
about me
but
S O M E T I M E S
it is

and I deserve my dreams, too

choosing
your own happiness
is not selfish
and W A N T I N G
is enough

Golden Afternoon

My blooms cannot be bought

I will not be plucked and cut
the best parts of me
dropped into a Limoges vase
and forgotten again
on the dining room table

you only want what we could become
now that I've grown thorns
and know how to fill a room
with the heady scent of intention

you never recognized
my buds in their most infantile form
so why would I give you golden afternoons
when you couldn't weather the storm?

Pick Me

The idea of this came to me in a dream one night and I know that sounds cliche but let me tell you all the ways how the thing I used to have looked like silver filigree from the outside; something beautiful soldered together on the surface but missing its purpose; the story of how I became a hollowed-out tree when I gave you all the best parts of me, and in the end it was I who poured the gasoline *but I'm not sorry for playing with fire*.

You see I had to do it if I ever wanted to know what it's like to be the one with the royal flush, revealed in a rush of no one else's expectations but my own. For too many years I refused to grow up until I stopped chasing my own shadow and made a really long-distance phone call to myself from the other side of the nursery window and stopped having lies for breakfast. What's a fairy tale without a happy ending? Isn't that what we were chasing at the starting line?

When happiness reigned it wasn't real, only you feigning importance and me pretending to know how to play house like cleaning the mercurial mess we made all over the floor that wouldn't stay still long enough to sweep it under the rug for the hundredth time. I could only keep pretending I was fine for so long before the hairline cracks you made in me would start splintering out like lightning, glimpses in microseconds of another life I could have if I just made myself small enough to fit inside the word "believe"; that if Alice could do it, I could also believe as many as six impossible things, and maybe one of those things would end up being the dream of who I was always **meant to be**, but when you tack the word "**with**" onto the very end of that sentence it takes on a whole new meaning, and I'm sorry if that hurts these are just feelings and *fuck* even I sometimes don't know how to keep breathing under the crushing weight of something like that, telling the person who used to hold your forever in his palms just to keep it warm that you were gonna have to take that back now because it didn't belong to him anymore.

That's the kind of door I never wanted to open because I couldn't bring myself to hurt you but there comes a point in a person's life when she's lived too long for someone else that she has to start picking herself first this time so you see I couldn't sacrifice me again. I knew it had to be you when the sound of my own name started tasting bitter coming out of your mouth; when I faded to black like the end of a bad B-list movie; how I ripped myself apart at the seams just to see if there was anything still left in me. I don't expect you to un-derstand why I Houdinied myself out of this but through the chains on my wrists, my words began to feel more like oxygen than you ever did, and those dreams tasted like the colors of fall that would inevitably burn me in the best way if I could just keep scaling the clouds of each new day, to find a way to exchange one forever for another, climb inside the words I was writing and stay. Stay. *"Please stay,"* you said.

I'm sorry, but this time I have to pick me instead.

You Asked for This

You couldn't recognize the truth
even when it roller skated by in a pink fringe jacket
swigging champagne
and blasting 80's love songs
from a broken boombox
skip skip skipping
over the parts about uncertainty
and spilling little epiphanies all over your plans

honey,
subtlety was never my thing
and I guess noticing the signs
was never yours

The Crash

You called me *broken* once.

now I realize you were right

that sometimes I do break
but only in the way
a wave crashes along the shore
rushing in powerfully and forcefully
the greatest strength in the retreat
softer than it was before

You May Have Won the Battle

For too long
I made a home among shadows
owning an archetype of the tired lost traveler
dirt caked under my nails
and scars on my heart
thinking these were the things
I'd always carry and bear
that made me, shaped me
drowned out the sound of my own voice

it's so much harder this time around
to write from the trenches
when silence is no longer a choice

Self-Care

It's funny how comfortable I became
once I allowed myself the space to breathe and be
to settle a little deeper into my being
no longer needing to rip it all back
in the exposed blood and bone I used to call home
but gently scrub at it with a terry cloth rag
and let the saltwater cleanse me instead

So tonight
I'll wax poetic from the tub
washed out in cerulean blue
and scrub off all the little pieces
left of you

Love Thyself

Today Eros found me
sitting on a grandiflora rose
inscribed with cursive letters
intricacies of the deepest parts of me
drawn toward the point of a pen

he pulled my head from the clouds
and whispered love notes in my ear
promises of the shades of red
I've been dreaming of

his words filled my mouth
like the taste of a kiss with a sugar rim
and transfigured my longing
and the question marks stuck in my throat
into lyrical prose
from overstuffed lipstick-stained envelopes

Return to Sender, they said
and those words
were all I needed to hear

Vows

How strange it is
to both want love
and fear it at the same time

of how so raw a thing
could change a person

and sometimes
"*for better*"
means "*for worse*"
when your worth
must come first

Withered

We used to be in full bloom
but even I
can still appreciate the dried flower
for what it once was

She/Her

I spend my days
contemplating
all the ways I can become
as I come undone
learning to love the only one
that's ever been with me
building a new identity
compounded and unbound
a word wrapped in pronouns
I'm still learning to pronounce

Little Girl Lost

I'm sorry for all the times
I never showed up for you
and left you with scars
instead of stars
yet your constellation eyes
still shine even now

you've held on to that magic
locked it away until the time felt right
until you knew you were safe
knowing I'd come back someday
and scoop your frail body
pressed into mine
and thank you for holding the light for so long

your mind has been shaken
though your faith never was
and I'm sorry for all of the pain I have caused

hold my hand in the dark
let me refill your cup
it's high time you've remembered
it's time we wake up

Finding My Footing

I crash-landed so quietly
in a field of Carolina flowers
that you never
even
noticed
the wreckage
between sips of scotch
content to sit in your world
while I had one foot in another
letting the past burn slow
and savoring a new sunrise
the flavor of hope

On the Eve of Creation

Maybe we were always ill-fated
and I just chose to ignore it
recoiling instead
deeper into the garden
where ripened truth beckoned
that tasted sweeter on my lips
than you ever did

you can keep your rib

I'd rather have knowledge

Excavation

The path to self-discovery is just a lesson in archeology
it was always there
buried beneath years of dust and debris
feeling the heartbeat of freedom just above the surface
distant and muffled but vibrating deep
slowly
piecing these bones back together
until they could stand once more
strong enough to dig my way back out

The Day I Left Sleepy Hollow

They can take so much if you let them
when they reach into you with hungry hands
scooping out your parts like it's Halloween
and those chips on your shoulders
can turn into cracks in your soul
but the powerful thing about breaking
is it lets the light in
and dreams
are not so easily stolen

Would You Like Sweetener with That?

The best kind of date
is just words and coffee
hours with myself over clicking keys
pulling myself apart for the thousandth time
just to see if the heart
ever learned how to play nice with the head
pouring too much milk & sugar in my coffee again
attempts to cool it to a palatable temperature
but I just get burned by my candor instead

The Forecast

I wrote you a love poem
so that I could look back one day and say,
"This is how I loved you then"

immortalizing all the scenes that came between
the meeting and the knowing and the becoming
to read over these words and sit with them
in all the moments that came next
tossed up in the storms
and soothed into stillness after the rain
to know that I loved once
and I could always love again

Baa Baa Black Sheep, How Do You Like Your Tea?

I took my tea alone at the table again
murky Earl Grey gone ice cold
as summer rain fell in a slow drizzle of truth
while you were passed out on the couch
and this upended upheaval fell
↓THIS SIDE DOWN↓
spilling my peacekeeper dreamsleeper contents
all over the dining room floor
arranged in formalities
I couldn't conform to anymore

and when you asked why
I could only reply

No amount of chamomile
left in the cabinet
could ever
put a black sheep
back to sleep

S.O.S.

I was a sinking ship once
emotions flooding me
before my watertight doors could close
while my heart
ever vigilant and loyal
vowed to go down with that ocean liner
until hope arrived in a life raft
and put us both in glass
for safe keeping

but what good is a ship in a bottle
that only yearns to explore this world
searching for buried treasure?

Better Days

There will be days where you will be the badass bitch in a power suit, enveloped by an unstoppable energy conjured from every goddess in the pantheon. These days come and go, suddenly followed by long lethargic weekends of peanut butter ice cream and pajamas, each limb rooted firmly into old couch cushions, the ones with the yogurt stains your daughter made; the ones you never even bothered to clean up. Maybe because on the days she's not there, it reminds you that there is some- one else who still loves you. Little remnants of love that linger when it's just silence and stillness.

There will be days at work when you can only hold your shit together long enough to just make it to the bathroom to cry in private. Days at home when you pull into your garage and immediately tears start flowing. Days when you catch a memo- ry unexpectedly in the city you've been trying to escape. Days when social media stretches you like a measuring tape, and you come up short every time. Days when you immediately retreat to bed sheets.

There will be days where you stare at yourself in the mirror and marvel at your resilience, your brilliance, your rebirth, and your beauty that took the better part of three decades to finally set free *and believe*. And there will be days where you cry to yourself in that same mirror because she feels like the only one that ever consistently shows up; so you hold her gaze a little while longer just to feel held by something, anything, trans- fixed on glass so sleek that you can't tell where you end and she begins.

But you must remember: *both are you*. At your best, you are beautiful. And at your worst? *You are still beautiful.*

Both are needed, and both are always whole.

Final Sale

Your love
taught me how to transcend my pain
and in loving you
I found myself again

I just never expected the cost to me
would come at the expense of us

Equidistant from the Heart

Yes
two halves can make a whole
but sometimes
they're just two halves

Nail Holes

I took down all the pictures today
the ones of us sitting static
on the underside of a moment
you know,
the ones framed in good faith and hope
and bright futures that were just too fragile
for us to hold

I thought it would hurt more than it did
to pluck memories from the wall
one by one
each photograph
restarting little movie clips in my head
and sound bites of laughter
echoing down the hallway
childlike ghosts of a bygone love

but instead
the place where I thought the pain would be
where grief used my heart like a drum circle
has been exchanged for stillness and reflection
contemplation and appreciation
for the gifts this love has given
for the hard lessons that brought strength
and the profound wisdom that holds hands with gratitude
skipping rope with peace

I took those pictures down today
but the memories?

the memories can stay

Sincere Apologies

Some part of me will always be tied to you
as sure as there are stars in the sky
because of the light we made
from the love we gave
but I have changed
I am not the same
I must flow and grow and shift
I have been given a chance to rewrite this
and although we remain connected
I get to choose not to be defined by you
or the choices I have made
because I've been forged in the fire
and I would have burned if I had stayed

When You Open Your Mouth & No Sound Comes Out

Speak.
A word that used to shake me
something I thought would break me
but instead, it took my soul
and wrung it out like a sponge
letting all the fear
and judgment
and expectations
that didn't belong to me
spill out all over the page
shaping inkblot thoughts
of what I was not
only what I could become

A Royal Flush

Wandering, wondering
I slipped into the last chapter of a story
with the flash of a white-tailed dream
disappearing
like a magic trick in reverse
through a top-hat hole
and the question burned crimson,
"Just how deep does the rabbit hole go?"

stumbling, tumbling
I found my name at the bottom
beating faintly like a dying star
in a garden of white roses
crudely painted a muted red
their brilliance covered up
in that heavy cracked hue

concealing, revealing
we sat playing poker with card sharks
your spades stacked against my clubs
while I hid the ace
but I was never very good
at masquerade charades
and putting up a front

my success story
was never one of knaves and knights
or your suit of diamonds on my finger
silver and gold
when I was always destined
to rule alone

queens like these
wear their heart on their sleeve
and mine told the tale
of madness in the dark

so I'm sorry for the way
the chess pieces moved
but the only way out
was off with your heart

Session Timeout

I got an error message today at work that read, *"Due to inactivity, your session has timed out and you have been logged off,"* and it got me thinking—about all those times in this marriage that I crept out the back door of my brain and my heart refused to stay, but my body didn't know any better. My body, this form melting like a candle over you just to keep you warm while I . . . I just kept burning.

Due to inactivity, it said, *you . . . have been logged off*. Like I had a power switch you could flick to turn me back on, this machine, this technological thing reduced to life on repeat only to please the parts of you that were so unbecoming, but I was too blind to see what it was doing to me; how I had changed and shifted in the wrong direction, hydroplaning all over this love until I realized that the crash is what would save me. It first had to break me before it could wake me and take me back home to a place I could be alone with the parts of me you scattered all over the road.

And the thing is that I may not know where to go from here, but it seems pretty clear to me that looking backward isn't the best way to see what's ahead of you, so I'm going to keep pounding these keys and typing my fury until it all spills out of me. I'll come back online fully present and plugged in to something new this time, because I was never meant to be yours and you were never mine, and what I'm coming to realize is to get the right thing, sometimes you have to let the wrong thing go even if it's all you know, protective like a wool coat in winter until you notice the moth holes and threadbare collar but you keep . . . holding . . . on because it's the only thing you've got, and you'd rather shiver in the street than acknowledge what we're not.

But me? *I'm done playing house, and it's ok to log off.*

Now Boarding

I am not a flyover state
I am the destination

Building the Temple

You stand now
in the wake of broken vows
with every past version of myself
that never knew how

I take your words
and her words—
mix them into mortar
into newfound foundations

and the grit of that sand
feels like power in my hands

On Rare Occasions

It doesn't happen often but there are still times
I trip on the punctuation of a day
and fall into the arms of a good time
all too willing
to drown again in wine

now when I drink too much
I don't linger like a fool in a drunken haze
that fog only ever existed
to get me lost in the first place
just to force me to find my way back

now when I drink too much and start spilling secrets
I don't feel the sting of regret
because I know how much truth exists there
and I let it animate me instead

now when I drink too much
I still reach for my phone
but open the notepad instead of your number
and read poems in amusement the next morning
I have no recollection of ever writing

now when I drink too much
I think too much
and just call it a lesson in limits
and an exercise in expression

Give & Give

Resilience, hope, strength:
these are the only things I carry now
after I poured out the last drops of my love
from a cup you never refilled

Editor-in-Chief

Right now it all feels like a rough draft
I am continually reworking and editing
redlining and erasing
inserting and indicating the imperative importance
of the subjective subjunctive of my many moods
fraught with possibility one moment
and grammaticle erors in the final draftt teh next

I suppose
that's why I proofread everything too many times
and invariably stumble upon the inevitable lesson
so long as I keep underlining
what still needs work

I Make My Own Art

When the flipbook stops
that is the moment I escape the page
and exist

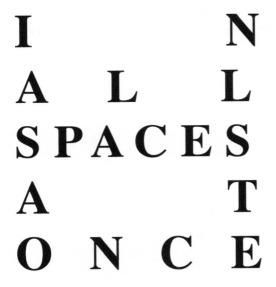

as a rough sketch

        gone

               rogue

Things They Failed to Mention about Divorce

1. The subtle sting of that statement on intake forms reading, "Please list your emergency contact"
2. Procrastination arriving in the form of cleaning the house for the 5th time instead of plucking wedding photos off the wall
3. The agony of waiting in this weird hibernation period in between who you were and who you will become
4. Extra trips to the grocery store because your mind is too preoccupied by the past to remember milk and eggs
5. Late-night glasses of wine to coax the words out from hiding because you can't face the truth without the 3rd glass of liquid courage
6. Distractions in the form of extra scheduled events, play-dates, and workouts to cover up the thoughts that rot in the box of his things you still haven't cleaned out
7. Baths in a quiet house on the nights your kid isn't home and yet the peace you so hungrily craved before now feels starving somehow
8. Popping the first seam on a heart you stitched closed long ago before everything fell apart
9. Letting the quiet fill all your hollow parts and sitting with it
10. Acknowledging your pain and making friends with all the ghosts in your bed
11. Changing your entire name and seeing your power reflected back to you in inky letters on those same intake forms you used to hate
12. Packing up the photos but letting the memories stay

13. Greeting the 8.0 version of you that knows how to let the world pour out of her in words instead of bearing that weight on her shoulders

14. Saving money on groceries

15. A glass of red poured between friends over rich conversation and the support that feels like intoxication one sip in

16. Unpacking the box of his memories you shoved in the back of the attic of your mind and appreciating them for what they were: beautiful things that live on forever in a moment in time

17. Long baths while your favorite movie, the one he never wanted to watch together, plays in the background

18. Realizing your first marriage was really just a rough draft of what you were always meant to have

19. Gifts that finally arrived from backorder: strength, resilience, independence, confidence, and self-love

20. Owning your narrative and penning your whole story and your own perspective, shaded in the indescribable color of new beginnings

Striations of a Scallop

I used to think my nickname
for my birth name, Michelle,
was ironic:
Shell
this tough outer covering of an animal
or the empty part left behind;
calciferous, tough, protective

my adolescence was punctuated by this idea
always hesitant to reveal
any fragile or deep part of myself
afraid to uncover or share my truth
with anyone
except for the protected pages of a notebook

it wasn't until years later
when I had learned some life lessons
begun to heal my pain
accepted my own love
that I appreciated and understood
the beautiful duality of that word

the seashell may be rough or broken on one side
but turn her over
and you expose her counterpart to the light
the smooth and opalescent interior
holding all the secrets of her being
that just needed to be brave enough
to be cracked open

Before the Hearing

I was a creature of habit
addicted to the creature comfort
of a warm body next to me in bed
filling my belly at times with peace
while others found me fasting and silent
across an ocean of sheets
crying in showers
locking myself in bedrooms
and excusing myself
to fall apart quietly
slowly
dissolved
lest I worry anyone
with the frivolity of tears and truth
when there was so much else to tend to

over time the universe calculated
a good faith estimate
of how to measure what was left
from the tender inner world
where I sat waiting and praying
while Atlas kept pressing further upon my shoulders
as if submitting
had anything to actually do with a man

I toss and turn so much sometimes
because I'm still trying to get comfortable
with the way these lessons feel on my skin
knowing my greatest learning
has been the unlearning
of these patterns I'm in
and how it now feels for once
to be madly in love with me
but still married
to comfort zones and safety

Letting Go Looks Like

Sad girl days on the couch under the armor of a fleece blanket / a second helping of baklava / reorganizing the linen closet at 10 pm / putting off projects for months until a random afternoon on a Tuesday / unintentionally skipping meals / crying in parking lots, bathrooms, and closets / scrolling social media for hours / pulling the curtains back / deep breaths / washing the yoga pants you've been living in for days / taking yourself on a dinner date / reading a good book, uninterrupted / hands slicked over with paint / smiling at yourself in the mirror / loving the way your dark eyes still hold light / laughing again

Fever Dream

Fever dreams are curious things

one whisked me away
as I nodded off
over books and background noise
and woke up on the same couch
where I had just fallen asleep

you were there
your head in my lap
apologies tumbling out of your mouth
all the things you never said
all the times I was never seen
all the things you couldn't give to me
in all their beautiful simplistic necessity

"Come here," you said
pulling me to my feet
sensing my need
as we stood in the living room
beneath the parrot painting I hung when you left
the one you would have hated
on the whitewashed fireplace I did myself
the one we always had plans to repaint
together

it was there
in the empty living room of my mind
catharsis and closure
managed to find me and release me
like a slow exhale
from your ghostly memory

your arms tight around my body
giving me the one thing
I always needed
but could never request:
to simply be held
no questions asked

Red Ink & Final Decrees

I never knew what the last piece would be
when I reached the end
of this pivotal part of my story
until the eve of everything
found me awake four hours too early
not with the heart and head
going at it again
(they had already broken bread)
or worry or dread or grief
having already made my peace
with all those messy houseguests
that couldn't take a hint
but with a vision
like some wispy apparition
pulling back the veil of the unseen
beckoning
to let me peek behind that velvet
in curiosity and bewilderment
at the words upon the wall:
finie
finite
fertig
finalizada
terminada
finished

and so
I pick up the pen
and eagerly
begin
again

Superbloom

*My mind blooms in technicolor plumes
when the downpour of words
flows from my fingertips*

and in those letters lies salvation

The following was written in 2007, and is an excerpt from a blip of truth revealed between the pages of a lengthy journal, which I later realized was always destined to become a memoir.

2007

I want a transformation:
mind, body, and spirit

maybe then
someone will tell me I'm beautiful
and I can believe it

maybe then
I can believe
in the concept of love

maybe then
I can love myself

2022

Years ago
a part of me wrote a prayer
in a Microsoft Word journal

encapsulated a moment
so poignantly painful
that fifteen years later
I would rediscover her long forgotten words
that made my mouth fall open in the revelation
that I unknowingly manifested
e v e r y t h i n g
that followed

A Songbird's Strength

I used to hide my sacred texts
roll them up into the hollow bones
of an inky songbird with one broken wing
but no shortage of melodies
flapping restless against the wire door
until the hinges came loose
from too much frictioned truth
a trajectory arching up and out towards purpose
becoming both
the secrets within these four walls
and the breach of its whispered corners

Intentions

Through the midnight hour
I stand
staring at everything I had to burn
in favor of everything I have built
and choose to sing
of my own sovereignty

Stay

If I stayed
I never would have known how change tastes
or how the feel of growth settling into skin
allows the heart to open
lets the light in
and all those parts of me I thought I had to be
to fold backwards into conformity
into an illogical ideological antiquated part I had to play
of the stereotypical archetype by day
moonlighting as authenticity
would only bring me to my knees to pray
open my eyes to all the ways
I was falling apart in slow motion
surviving on an outdated notion
that safety and comfort equaled happiness squared
but my dreams were never there
so I traded my fear for strength
decided I too could travel great lengths
stretched along the belt line
to reach what was always fated as mine
and forgive my past for such unkindness
barter it instead for forgiveness
be more mind and soul
less fragmentation, more whole
to transplant my roots
so I could really grow

I never could have stayed in that place
because now I know
what it means to take up space

For the Time *Be*ing

You asked me if
T   H   I   S
(she gestured wildly)
was just a phase

if words were something
to be replaced with disinterest
and cast aside like little paper airplanes
with bent wings that couldn't fly

and I said no without thinking
for how could I ever one day
just decide to stop breathing?

Cockpit

At first
it felt like a crash landing

now I realize it was really
just a perfectly calibrated arrival

My Wild

I don't know
how a thing so wild
became a wildflower

The Library Lounge

There is a rotunda room here
just like the one in my head
where I saw us sitting
holding hands over coffee-stained pages
overstuffed chairs that swallow you up
floor-to-ceiling windows
revealing a painted mountain view
and damask drapes
tied back with thick tasseled rope
an inviting space with books reaching the rafters
welcoming me as one of their own
beckoning to becoming

they don't know just how far
I've already fallen from the shelf
or how many old endings I had to edit
before I could write the final draft

they don't know just how close I am
to the last chapter of this first epoch
with so many more to come

Rebirth

Mythical mistress
painted in the colors of early dawn
a silhouette against a sky on fire
reborn in effervescent light
the true self finally unearthed
exhumed
exalted

The Journey

I am just a woman
with a notebook and a dream
trying to free
the wild magic within me

A Revolution of Revelations

Just as the earth
spins on its axis
and feels her power
grow from the inside,
I will lean a little more
into mine

Crossing the Threshold

Imagine
the tenderly cracked spine of a book
cradling things that cannot be held
only felt
omnipotent hands penning the world
to pin-mount the thorax of a thought

encapsulate an elusive emotion
painted in nascent prisms of wispy light
refracted beauty in radiant colors
that stain the mirrorball mind

hues of translucent pastel
enveloping in an embrace
that feels like warm chamomile tea
spilling over me
healing and soothing
the restless, weary wanderer
setting up camp for the night
in clouds of poetry

a mermaid moon flips her tail
in a flash of scaled brilliance
just enough to flick a star overhead
sending a cascade of rosy maple moths
scattering secrets down below
while I rush to catch every story
that eager hands can hold

how fulfilling it feels to dip my hands
into imagination's painted truth
knowing that while it is a part of me
it was always meant
for you

Que Sera Sera

I cry so much these days
…from gratitude
from love
from *h e a l i n g*
from hope
from joy
from energy anchored
in the gravity
of   this
present
moment

I   ex *i s* ist
only
in the now
in a constant
flow
of
beautiful
s u r r e n d e r

Aperture

At some point
I stopped taking so many pictures
to preserve my memories
and started writing instead
choosing to encapsulate the beauty of a moment
through sonic texture and expansive descriptions
of black and white sepia toned technicolor
low light back-lit overexposed subtleties
overshadowed grainy noise shouted above the rest
a little out of focus
always on purpose

at some point
I got so frustrated with f-stops
and the way the moon and I both appeared on film
that I *F*-stopped believing in cameras

some things require much more space
to portray an accurate depiction
and there is no lens available
to capture this much light

The Huntress

There's been a lot of talk lately
about arrows and targets
and making your mark
with the kind of badassery
born from a bow & arrow
but I'm no Robin Hood
just a modern day Artemis
in a pair of stiletto boots
with a quiver full of truth
a wildfire ripping through wildflowers
the storm surge in a hurricane
whiplash in a crown
mismanaged mischief always afoot
unconcerned with the sound a bullseye makes
or my arrow's precision
but ever-insatiable for the thrill of the hunt
and what may emerge
from the edge of the woods

The Door of Possibility

It is not the road less traveled
but the one left undiscovered
a vagrant wanderer
not knowing where you're going
only that you must

it is ripping up your roots
and getting used
to the way "chance" feels in your body
parched for truth and starving for adventure

it is an ominous mystery desperate to be solved
trying every which way in the maze
and wanting to get lost

it is digging up your power from bare earth
hands tired from the fight
but carrying it gently toward the finish line

it is fragility made combustible with lift & thrust
wings sprouting, earth shaking
expanding and unfolding into a mind on fire

it is a one-way street that ends in a door
and the way the knob rattles at first turn
fear if you step forward, regret if you don't

how your heart pounds in your chest
while the past fades to black
hands pressed against iron
now there's no turning back

The Schematics of Stars

Irony becomes me with a Gemini sign
once silent and quiet
now a master communicator, jack of all words
talkative & chatty, working the room like a pro

I am the sincere storyteller choosing to craft timelines
imagery and movement with my fingers
doing an intricate dance of diction
that flows like rivers converging onto parchment
for I speak with wild hands
and a wise pen traversing the twisted highways of paper
precise navigation of blank lined pages
Magellan could never match

I am the astronaut shooting up like a rocket
trailing billowing, mushroomed rainbow plumes behind me
with stories shaped from stars
the shadowed corners of the universe dotted with ringed planets
like beautiful eyes in the dark glowing bright white light
a heat burning through my veins so hot
relieved only from supernovas of ink
exploding onto paper

I am the explorer with a fierce and unwavering belief
in buried treasure & ghost ships
in mermaids & sunken civilizations
fearlessly sailing deeper into open water
with stories trawled from the expanding, endless unknown
a navy so rich and dark it permeates the mind
birthing beautiful movement only I can see
these countless visions that pull at my heart
and illuminate my soul

I am the witch
healer of shadows
hands digging into dirt
roots growing in infinite directions
with stories pushed forth slowly from soil
cradled in the palms of Mother Earth
this raw, organic energy that cannot be contained
a superbloom in a cracked & scorched desert
for where there is life,
there is hope

each story
a tiny, tender newborn of syllables & syntax
metaphors & metamorphosis
diction & dreams

each story
another layer peeled back
from the expanse of an ancient soul
with so much left to say

When the List of Demands Becomes Too Great to Ignore

My hand is well versed in automatic writing
it autonomously draws an unconventional life
a feral spirit ripping free
that was never meant to be
one size fits all

I want to be outer limits
out of bounds
an undiscovered planet generating its own light
pulling others into orbit
the eternal verities of my very gravity
expressed effortless in a void
that knew nothing but nothingness
before my Big Bang arrived
with her big mouth and even bigger words
demanding to be heard

"Speak! Rise!
Make an honest effort this time!
All the other versions are watching
with bated breath
just to see how far you get."

with words, wisdom, and will . . .
hah

guess I'm a triple threat

The Inevitable Combustibility of Shrinking Violets

When the wallflower
becomes the wildflower
I am an unstoppable force
Night Gladiolus blooming in the dark
spicy fireflowers of fuming smoke
tiny tendrils stretching
reaching not for stars
but the whole damn sky
petal pressed against the moon
(tired of the sun and his arrogance)

chasing divinity into infinity
lit up by the chase
no longer asking, just taking
expanding unraveling
like the creation of my own universe
in dollhouse miniatures

cradling new beginnings
from where it all began
to stretch
and bask
and be
what took a thousand years
to finally set free

how foolish you were to think
your walls could ever contain me

Incubator

There are certain words I cannot keep
the *how* and *when* do not make a home here
only *what* and *why*
the intrinsic unquestionable
building a nest upon which I rest
impossible beliefs
becoming effortless over time
and newness cracked from eggshells
I once thought stone
left alone
to flourish and grow

no
I was never pushed from the nest

it was *always* my intention
to jump

Choose Your Own Adventure

I'm only here for a little while
and I want to get the most out of it;
I want to paint a sunset on my skin
brighten my inner world

to gather stars in my hands
swallow them whole
feel that heat
as it burns down my throat

to lasso the clouds
carried off at dusk
sailing into my own storybook
lit with dreams and melodies and love
carving happiness from chance
and smearing out the fear
with ink-stained fingertips

I'm only here for a little while
and I choose songs instead of silence

Firestarter

I dance through flames with purpose
just to feel the weight of my being
beat fierce through channeled brilliance
not afraid to burn once more
reduced to furling edges
withered up in smoke and ash
certain
that I will always rise again
and flames
could never burn away my truth

Chapter Two

I love who I'm becoming
full of light
full of change

I love this new version
forming on the page

Intentionally Untitled

You said, *"you've lost it!"* in a fit of fury
a diamond ring
a Mrs. title
the mind
control
and I couldn't help but laugh
knowing what I know
that these things were never lost
so much as they were
let go

Level Up

I unzip my skin
hitch a ride on the wind
and I'm carried off in blue;
a thousand miles away
from the me I used to be
never to be pulled from truth

Invocation

There is a place in existence
(perhaps Mt. Olympus)
a wild and wondrous whimsy of sorts
that must be invoked and spoken into being
from the heart's only language of intention

the location doesn't matter
but it is here the muses gather
and bicker (eloquently) over me
as they clamor to be the one
who comes through next
each with arms overflowing
eagerly bestowing their precious gifts
wisdom by divine design
that transcends these beguiling concepts
of space and time

and today it seems
they're all running the show
making room for magic
beauty
strength
via effortless flow
of an expanding soul
that these days knows nothing of limits
and everything of growth

If You Open Me up like a Dollhouse

I grew up in the 90s
so it stands to reason
I should live to see my 90s
when this body becomes nothing more
than a cold-cut cadaver
slit open to reveal a slice of open dollhouse
and all its compartmentalized rooms
decorated in the splendor and wonder
that life continually fed me

a vaudeville show in a three-act attic
where dust becomes gold sequins
sparkling over everything
magicians and acrobats and comedians
pulling song lyrics from the chimney
tumbling and leaping through the air
finding light and laughter
even when no one was there

this middle layer though
is a bit more intriguing
with wooden stairs where the bottom step creaks
rooms on either side that are a bit musty
like my grandmother's shawl
and old forgotten Passover Haggadahs
a seder of my life spoken in Hebrew
that wanted wine instead of water
expectations I expected to leave behind
in favor of climbing further
into the attic of my mind

the first floor finds me
reaching into rooms
to feel the flowered wallpaper
and the mess of barbies on the floor
each one
with their hair chopped haphazardly
from scissors that felt anything but safe
where the doors stayed closed for too long
but the nightlight was always left on
so the magic could still find me
even in the dark

cadavers are curious things
and I hope when the time comes
for me to leave one reality behind
in favor of a Greater Bright
that I will go willingly
and peacefully into the night
with my three-ring circus show
born from the greatest truth
I ever had the honor
to come to know

Home: /hōm/

noun
1. A haven where stories & memories are created.
2. Frequencies of peace, safety, and love, manifested as a physical form.
3. The feeling of setting yourself free.

Turn

You wonder why I always have such a love affair with autumn
bewitched by the transformation of painted leaves
that look like fire cradled in my palms
but it is not so much the season that grasps me . . .

. . . it is the very idea of change itself

Vernal Equinox

The very rebirth of my being rushing full tilt on the heels of a
life suspended; wild and windy, carried off in all directions in a
billow of tempestuous storm clouds; ink and paint spilling over
earth in spiraled spectral colors, the weathered grey peeled
back slowly like a bandage revealing a new hue of sky called
"*Soft Return*"; familiar whispers slipping through willows; a
guiding birdsong in the early dawn still drenched in stars and
silhouettes; slow unfolding mornings that feel like forgiveness;
the hairline fractures of a speckled robin's egg in the shape
of resistance cleaving into freedom; the first invigorating
sip of nectar from budding sustenance; awakening, flowing,
changing, becoming, growing; rough beginnings and soft
endings; a gasp of first breath after too much darkness;
light swelling on the corners of what came before, leaving
a trail of tangible magic in its wake; a second chance for a
new beginning, naked, bare, and stripped back in crowning
resilience; an eternal spring blooming from the starting line of
my spirit.

The Body Reveals the Book

If we are the average of the five people
we spend the most time with
(or things in my case)
then these days I must be
a four-year-old in pink footie pajamas
babbling bedtime stories of ever-expanding wonder
a friend with crystalline perspective
able to temper the boiling pot before it all burns
a loyal dog trailing from room to room
ever willing to drop unconditional love
at the foot of my altar
the lyrical interpretation of vinyl records
releasing the chaos from my body
thick notebooks of letters that have no qualms
about illuminating the darkest shadows

both adult and child
solitude and community
human and animal
silence and sound

every secret and every veracity
ripped from the book
intentionally
eternally
unbound

Intrepid Introductions

I went from
small
and silent
to a wanted
wild
riot

These Days

For the first time
I am learning how to hold myself
how to make space
how to give myself the things I crave
how to want and how to take

these days
I feel more like a woman
and less like a girl

these days
I feel less like the shell
and more like the pearl

Love Spells

I saw you at the apothecary today
the one we used to come to
with its tins of tea lining the walls
one for every ailment imaginable
and some to manifest a little magic
sprinkled with cinnamon and rose petals
herbal blends for bruised hearts
like ours

your eyes
looked like the weathered hulls of ships
cresting over a gray sea
lost
in empty pleasantries

she saw me before you did
her own blue eyes brightening
shouting *Mommy!*
as she ran for a hug

now I sit alone
sipping rooibos and honey
playing my piano of keyboard letters
making music from what channels through
hoping one day we both find
the love we're looking for
left open
for something new

3 Wishes

To jump
without a shred of doubt
knowing faith will cradle the fall

To explore
in all directions
absolute sovereignty of self

To love
ferociously and fiercely
wielding my heart as the sword
finally freed from the stone

Note to Self

Looking inward
through the greenhouse glass
the solarium of your essence
in deep viridian
houses intuition and inspiration

this is the immortal sage garden
depth and dormancy
such a paradoxical paradise
of greenery and growth among the shadows

meadow phlox
a loud showy flower of candy-colored blooms
not yet rendered into this reality

your folklore is still unfolding
and such an exotic underground blossom
has already piqued my interest

Lady's Slipper Orchid

Cultivate me
the veracious garden that I am now
having been the drought
the famine
the storm
I yield now in merciful exaltation
passion born of patience
and tilt towards light
every plush petal
unfurled
presented
wanted
a radical and rare
full bloom of absolution

What's in a Name

I disagree
with Shakespeare's theory

names are anything
but irrelevant

to some
my old name is a prayer
blessings across an ancestral lineage
wrapped in the melody of that famous Beatles line
but I was never yours
and it never truly felt like mine

to me
over time it was a cage
with a songbird stuck inside
confined spaces and hollow bones
that knew no rhyme
no reason why
things had to be
so black and white

nothing stays the same
and the name became
a double entendre
synonymous with seashells
closed
sealed
yearning to be cracked open
taking the purpose
the powerful "why"
leaving only the exoskeleton behind

I never asked for what they called me
and if the only constant is change
then I *choose*
to have a siren song in my middle name
and a rebel of revelations in my first
here only to challenge the mundane
and make magic from my words

Natural Occurrences

I will not settle for barren rivers
stagnation
shallow stillness
or sedimentary remains

I was first carried quietly on the slow current
before smashing against rocks
cracked open
rinsed clean

I now daringly and adventurously
ride such necessary wild rapids
and flow with fate head on
into the gold rush of my own becoming

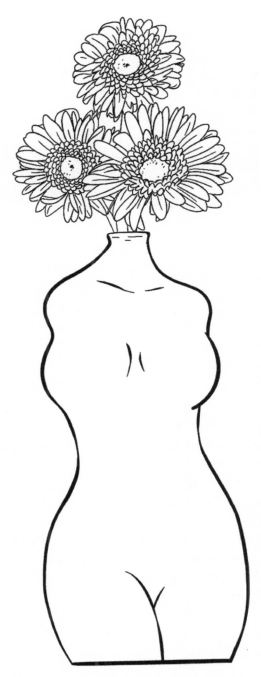

62

"It gives me joy to think
I have a pretty little girl
lovely as a golden flower;
Cleis, whom I so adore
I would not take all Lydia
nor Lesbos (even lovelier)
in exchange for her"
                    -Sappho

The following piece was written around seventeen years old,
twelve years before I had my first child. Over a decade later, I
rediscovered it in a box of my adolescent work and put the piec-
es together that I quite literally manifested my entire journey, as
well as my daughter, years before anything ever happened—and
yes, she was born with hyacinth blue eyes to two very surprised
brown-eyed parents. This poem stands as a testament to the
magic of the universe, the power of the written word, and the
mystery of such a miraculous rebirth.

Muse —*for Lilly*

I envisioned a Greek goddess
sheathed in cerulean satin
rippling like water across alabaster skin
outstretched arms encircling my waist
breathing life into my body
words surging to the surface
these uncovered treasures
buried in my brain

who knew she was something different
not yet a day old, swaddled in pink silk
stretching pudgy fingers
curled around my thumb
opening eyes like a blossoming flower
hyacinth color
sending me spinning into space
filling my mouth with stories
words to swallow and share

her first glimpse at the world
was always fated
as my rebirth

In the dumpster fire summer of 2020, as I listened to Taylor Swift's newly released **Folklore** *album, something sparked in me, and the inspired words flowed effort-lessly. This was the first poem I dared to pen in well over a decade, and she now breathes immortal as the last loving piece on page 143. I like to think Taylor's music and incredible talent for storytelling had a hand in that—energetically, magical-ly, musically. These final lines exist as a loving response to "Who Am I if Not an Artist," dedicated to the many versions of me that came before. It has always been— and always will be—stories and songs that unlock every door.*

Soul Revival

In my dreams I'm a traveler
slipping easily between tenses
where visions stack like layer cake
reveal her gilded form
holding the hem of her cotton dress
as she glides to the river's edge
wading, wanting
to be cleansed in its depths

her mouth in the shape of questions
that I still don't have any answers to
poignant and thorny
that make more tally marks on my heart

there was a beginning once
that would ripen into fruit
when I bought her faith with a single wish
but strayed too far from my post
as vigilante of newborn hope
abandoned the muse in a retreating wood
unknowingly extinguished the stars
and left only earth
crumbling underfoot

the whole time
her eyes still hang a welcome sign
arms raised to a high heaven

heavy with all the teardrop shaped promises
I always made but never kept
slippery when wet
elusive things I could never catch

she shows them to me
these little tenderlings
barely still breathing
soul revival, she calls it
like she is my church
and knows how to press her mouth
all the way up to God
to fast-track a soul back into its body
in poetry and words
washed in the tint of a Tennessee sky

they say it's bad luck to see yourself in a dream
and I know two cents can cost a lot these days
but that's not something I'm buying

her freedom was coiled around my belief
she, the escape artist
masterful magician
and I
her mere apprentice to that kind of enchantment
the overture to a show we hadn't practiced yet

this time promises pour out of her mouth
in a great crescendo of an embrace
the sound two halves of the same soul make
returned
to where we once belonged
inside a dream made whole
that was there all along

Press Play

Music has always been present in my life in a very intentional and impactful way. It has an incredible ability to create massive change within a person and can speak directly to the heart. The right kind of music can uplift, inspire, soothe, and heal. For this particular book and chapter of my life, this was that write kind of music.

"Lillies" | Huft
"Moonflower" | Lia Marie Johnson
"Wallflower" | Latir
"Shrinking Violets" | PHOX
"Lotus Intro" | Christina Aguilera
"Garden" | Nahko And Medicine For The People
"Mantras" | Ellen Winter
"Light On" | Maggie Rogers
"Believer" | Imagine Dragons
"Easy on Me" | Adele
"SUPERBLOOM" | MisterWives
"Back in My Body" | Maggie Rogers
"Decide to Be Happy" | MisterWives
"What Else Can I Do?" | Diane Guerrero, Stephanie Beatriz
"The Real Thing" | Audra Mae

Acknowledgments
The pangram of the book with many thanks
and even more names that typically no one sees
(but trust me, this is one you'll actually want to read)

There are many people who had a hand in helping me along this journey, who played a part in getting me from that initial late August to this spiritual Aquarian age in which my long-titled poems and I now congregate. There are too many to list as prayers upon the page, so I won't sing those ABCs of names. I'll just leave this here, open-ended, because many of you already know how your support has been received: mentally, emotionally, energetically. Honestly, I've probably written about you already or at least thanked you personally.

From the J.M. jaybird that first heard and helped me unearth my jailhouse rock from the rugged terrain of poetic obscurity to the Neverland *last name first* that rocket-launched this long-awaited rebirth, no pixie dust needed (your Titanic taught me the most and helped me build the Carpathia that rescued my throat). Literarily and literally, I can now look at all those facts and connect every timeline spun from the Charlotte of my past; and if you *stay, stay, stay* with me, perhaps future-you might decipher exactly what I mean by that. IMHO, I've gotten good at arcade games. My riddles are just treasure maps that could never be surpassed.

Once more around this track, back to the kindred Gemini twin who spent the night as I cried, afraid of every flickering red light in my life at the time, to the one, two, three editors redlining my rhyme along the way and every subtle shade of human who ever held space—both the ones who remain and the ones who couldn't stay. From the chance meetings and the late nights drowning in Schitts Creek, to the kind messages and every "Ew, David!" meme, everything persisting to simply be present and remind, "Chill out. Sit down. Everything will be alright, alright,

alright." (Spoiler alert: Matthew is on a future flight.) Suffice to say, best wishes, warmest regards, thanks (fill in the blank). You have all supported me in so many pulchritudinous, inexplicable, synchronistic ways.

Do not take offense if your reference does not arise. Give it time. My patient rhyming mind eventually runs clear. So drop a pin and be here in this amethyst and grey ambiguity until everything comes full circle in Cuban blue continuity. Those of you who see beyond my names need no formal standing ovation of overdone accolades. You were part of my growth, and your impact simply shows. Your return on Chapter Two's investment is quite evident in my prose.

And if you're new in town, yo-ho, hi, hello! This book is the first in a long line of verbose dominoes. My writing and I have evolved dramatically, so please take notes as this quick brown fox jumps over every lazy dog on my way to birth an entire vortex manifesto (the tennis shoes already know). This queen is emerging in a spelling bee of her own astute oratorical inferno. The flick of my wrist doesn't play discus with status quo; both fists already bloodied before breakfast slamming through six impossible plate glass windows. The powers that be are helping me with rewrites, scripting my life in *italics* and **bold**, co-piloting the pen and helping the words float. I only exist now in the (Cu)p-runneth-overflow. So hold your breath, anything goes. Where the next one lands . . . *only the universe knows.*

Photo by Ava Rymer (instagram.com/gingeredspice)

Maverick L. Malone is a writer, poet, and self-proclaimed "unearther of life." She believes in the magic of language as a powerful tool for alchemy, healing, and self-discovery. Though she has always considered herself a writer, her gifts were reignited in 2020, and she dove headfirst into manifesting her dreams. *Pressed Petals* is Maverick's literary debut, and she has plans for many more future publications. Currently, she lives in east Tennessee with her young daughter, Lilly.

You can find Maverick online at instagram.com/mavmalone and maverickmalone.com.